THANK YOU JOHN
FOR ALL YOUR SUPPORT
FOR SO LONG

ILLUSIONS
of
PERMANENCE

The Collected Poems
of Ron Ellison

ILLUSIONS
of
PERMANENCE

The Collected Poems
of Ron Ellison

edited by
Phil Bevis

CHATWIN BOOKS
Seattle, 2015

dedicated to my brother, Bud Sprague

Foreword

The first time I truly heard Ron Ellison speak,
he was in a circle of people sharing their feelings
after an evening of dance. He said, "This dance is
keeping me alive. You are keeping me alive." He was
speaking literally, not in metaphor. This scarred,
craggy man, so ill he was short of breath, fought
for air and went on to riff extemporaneously about
some of his feelings from that evening, about being
nearly dead, but finding life through movement and
the energy of the people around him. It was poetry,
coming from seemingly the most unlikely source.
Poetry—live, in the moment, and very real. He was
composing impromptu, off the cuff—and was later
asked by those present to write them down. Thus
many of the poems in this volume, which came from
similar spontaneous instances, truly embody the
oral tradition of poetry.

There have been many Rons over the years—many
of them, from all accounts, not easy to love. My Ron
is humble. I've no way to know if that humility is the
product of beatings at the hands of fate, spiritual
evolution, or a mix of the two.

Most of the time I've known Ron, he's been in poor
health, some days barely able to breathe. Often,
it has seemed like there are not many days left for
him, yet he is so alive, so passionate about today, this
moment, this dance, a person he just met. Though
any given day might be hard and dark, there is
always this moment, now. And on his worst day, he is
always here and present with you.

The least prideful person I know, Ron is the one who so often connects with baristas and busboys, who are often so surprised to be recognized as people with a smile and a kind word that they step towards this man's warmth, not letting the rough visage of a man who says "my face is not pretty" obstruct his humanity.

Ron is appreciative of the smallest of human interactions. An hour of time spent, that one dance shared, or being treated to a bowl of soup evokes both surprise and gratitude. He is rough-edged, yet his eyes are also often moist with gratitude and love.

He has been so surprised that anyone would take his writing seriously, or even read it, much less publish it. He would be so grateful and honored that you are spending time to experience and share his thoughts and work.

I hope that while reading, you understand that these poems were not written by Ron; they are a part of Ron, they are him. They are not a creation; they are an expression of a man whose greatest hope is that people "would see me."

It has been a great privilege to help Ron be seen. May the seeing touch your spirit.

Phil Bevis, Seattle, February 2015

Table of Contents

Part I - Reflections

It's True

I'm big
My face is not pretty
I walk funny, kind of flat-footed

I'm a Capricorn

It's my nature to plant every step
So it sinks deep as a posthole
And some people
Choose to be frightened
I wish they would see me

Think of a bison

Like the ones at Lascaux
Pretend you stand next to it
In the old forest
Dark and great
And you twine your fingers
In the hair on my shoulder
And fear nothing

See me

If the wind blows
Stand behind me

Ride my back
And no tiger would dare
Try to eat you

My size is a gift to you
My loneliness
I keep for myself

Having Things

Having things
just a distraction
a paper screen
with birds painted on it
to diffuse the light
of death
that insists on shining through
shadows
that only occur when I stand
between that glare
and my illusions of permanence
playing puppet theater
I think
I should make sure
to have things
to tie myself to
like a ship's mast
when sirens sing.

Alchemy

I can feel it.
My bones are humming
vibrating to a deeper resonance
the kind that makes dogs bark before an earthquake.
The kind that interrupts a whale's five-hundred-mile
whisper
or
an elephant's sub-audible
ten-mile conversation.
It is as if the world's molten core
has been struck like a mighty gong
that can be heard
at the edge of the solar system
If there were ears to hear.
Change is coming.
I stand on a cliff that changes into tiny glass beads
and then
crumbles into the ocean.
And I do not.
I too change.
I am vapor
I cannot fall.
All that I was to be
I have become.
The world and I together
are reaching our limitations.
There is little left for us to do
but leave the shells we have become
behind.
We must become something more
and something less

chalices of light and darkness
each
alternately flowing into
and becoming
the other.
I begin to understand the process
of turning lead
into gold.

A Murder of Crows

When I find you, it is always
far from the city
A raucous murder of crows
place a black border on a blue sky

I take it home and keep it
A memory of skeletal trees
with black punctuation

Of a poem much older than me

The Night Before I Move

No wonder people laugh
A fat man and a crippled dog
Seeking their fortune

The dog lies by the cozy heater
Not knowing the uncertain future
Her beloved master
Will soon subject her to

Bright dreams
Of fairy dust and love
Float behind the fat man's
Wounded eyes
As he welcomes
A flash of madness
In preference
To a slow slide to hell
And mediocrity

Soon

The walls will be gone
As if in a dream
And roads long abandoned
Will be dimly sought
Changed and chrome-plated

Intolerant

Of brittle bone
And sagging flesh
Held up by resurrected dreams
Long hidden
In the basement of his heart

It's fitting
That the dreams belong
To a younger man
They sizzle in a smaller version
Hidden inside
The rolls of lard
The layers of muscle
And deadly experience
Protected
As if by an older brother
Or caring uncle
Surrounding the naïve glow
With a hedge
Of wire and thorn

A glassy vision
In an armored car of flesh
Each nurturing the other
As they go forth
Together
With a crippled dog
And rusty van
A heart full of hope
And a gut full of fear
Sleep a while longer
Little dog
And forgive your master

Why Worry?

The trees
I left them and grubbed under logs
until I found a rock.

All the ages
of semen-stained time
line upon line
going nowhere
misspent by Onan.

They survive in delusions of grandeur
that are nothing
less than a drop in the ocean
in a time that does not exist.

How laughable
That I worry
when everything can't help but work right. There
is no other way
because a way does not exist.
All things
are
all ways
one.

Beelzebub

Disconsolate Demon
Lord of the Flies.
Small creatures of the world
with misery you leaven.
Sometimes wishing yourself a man
when all the little pests
get a little out of hand.

Orcas

Yesterday
I paced the orcas.
They had broken free
of the mosquito fleet
that doggedly followed them
like
rejected suitors
sullenly
hoping for a glance
or
an invitation to intimacy.
I sat
quietly singing
a song to lord Poseidon
thanking him
for the chance to offer my life to his children
knowing
they would accept
and then return it
forever changed
and larger
than it was ever designed to be.
And so
I paralleled their course
fifteen meters from the pod
three strokes
of the paddle
for every leap of theirs.
Four breaths
to every explosive one of theirs.
I have been a fisherman
and together

we have
in our time
left a red wake
of carnage and fullness
yesterday
I paced the orcas
last night
I dreamed of salmon
and not letting boats
crowd me off my tack.
I know
my brothers
sons of Poseidon
dream the same
as they laze
in the phosphorescent sea
lit by a pale moon.
They have forgotten me
but
I know
I will never forget them.

Alone

I come to this place
of sunlight
and serenity.

You are not here.
The silence we shared
is.

I share it with you
still.

The Letter

How can I
put years on a sheet of paper?
As I grow older
years fall at my feet like autumn leaves.
They surround me
brightly colored
discarded
useless.
How many have fallen since I've seen you?
I will bend down
and count them.

My Mother

Tear another chunk of pain
into an ever bleeding heart
and you will find me waiting
as I have waited
from the start.

Waiting
ever waiting
for the birds with mended wings
the rusty trikes
the worn-out bikes
football letters and things.

The things that you have forgotten
are the things that I hold dear.
They are all that I have got
now that you are never near.

You loved your sons
and the daughters you never had
and bittersweet
dusty memories
often make me sad.

From the Deep

The boat's name was *Star Lady*
her length in feet was 42.
a Radon-built salmon boat
painted orange and Portagee blue

We fished out of Crescent City, my brother and I
and even when the weather
was marginal
we'd ignore the old sailors' warnings,
take the boat out and try.

We would fish all four seasons
and stay out when others said
"It's too rough."
The local rednecks hated hippies
but said "the *Star Lady* boys are tough."

It happened late in the season.
It had been a shitty,
dirt-poor year.
We barely caught enough salmon
to pay for maintaining the gear.
"We're dragging our bait through the desert,
the fishing here's certainly dead."

So we bent our course out where it's deeper
and piled on 40 pounds
more lead.
We ran the gear down 100 fathoms
ran 15 baits per line
my brother's eyes
gave a twinkle
he said "This new tack suits me fine."

We shut the boat down and drifted.
I was so tired I slept like a log.
The next day the sun went away,
and we found ourselves fishing in fog.
"No sweat" says my brother
so we switch on the radar
a fisherman's seeing-eye dog.

I was watching the poles
for a nibble,
but admit I was half asleep
when all of a sudden
the jerking and pounding
told me something had taken our bait,
and bitten it hard,
way down deep.

It took a long time to bring the line in.
We wanted to retain our prey,
but when our catch finally broke the surface,
my brother and I stared in dismay.

Her hair was pale green.
It spread in the water
like a halo,
it was the longest I'd ever seen.
She was obviously bent,
from her rapid ascent
her painful distortion was obscene.

We were horrified
and not a little afraid.
What's a man to do
when his catch is a woman with gills
and a skin covered with scales
that shimmered
a bright steel-blue?

We cut her loose as fast as we could
and watched her sink back to the deeps
and this day
so many years later
the memory still gives me the creeps.

We didn't have much heart
for fishing
we turned the boat around.
We ran day and night
in obvious flight
until we could stand on dry ground.

My brother still fishes the *Star Lady*.
Fishes her
tough as tough can be.
But I assure you
my friend:
since that trip came to an end
he fishes without me.

Steel Tuna

I am only alive when I swim in the steel river
part of the iron food chain
a small opportunist amongst massive predators
feeding off their scraps of gas
and darting quickly away.
Swim upstream and die.
I live on a tributary of quietly moving asphalt
sluggish with traffic lights
and bottom-feeders.
I prefer to swim the mighty I-5

Or shoot the rapids of downtown Seattle.
I love it when the vinyl seat
squeaks with the sound of my asshole puckering
in fear,
as I leave a squirt of smoke from my tailpipes
to confuse a '63 Comet
driven by an old man
who obviously hasn't been taking
his Geritol.

Now
it is spring,
and I feel a strange new urge.
I have acquired tickets to ZZ Top
and feel a genetic compulsion to swim to The Gorge.
Perhaps I'll survive
and spawn.

Giant Killer

A tree.
Look at it as harmless
pretty
green latent death
to a man
killing a giant
for others who feed on its corpse
and pity it.
In a way incomprehensible
to a man
killing a giant
that can
and often does
kill him
as he kills
as easy
as living one more day of sweat
and passionate fear
of an angry giant
with a dead wooden heart.

Cats

Cats can be used for biofeedback.
Really.
My search for sacred sounds
did not originally include felines.
Chanting
Nepalese temple bowls
didgeridoos
The Mormon Tabernacle Choir
or John Mayall when I am on acid.
Good stuff
but not very predictable.
A cat now
that's the thing.
Ever pick a cat up when you are agitated?
Not a good idea.
Cats are like Zen masters
that claw you
instead of hitting you with a stick.
And the ability to produce
a purrrrrr
a breathy Yin Yang.
A cat is in your lap
and you are stroking it
without even knowing it
changing your tempo
in response
to subliminal cues
from a furry Buddha
who long ago
learned to achieve a state of no mind
while waiting
to catch a mouse

and is now kind enough to share
a sound that floats to Heaven
a burnt paper offering
with tranquil dreams written on it
for me.

Luck

I remember
working on my brother's fishing boat.
We went out in bad weather
a lot.

One day
as I untied the bowline
and jumped on board the departing boat,
Mike's wife,
she ran down the dock-ramp
out on the dock.
Her blond curls floating on the morning breeze
bright against the Payne's Grey sky.

"Don't go!
I had a dream last night!"
We pulled slowly away from the dock
and turned the boat out to sea.

That whole week-long trip
I cursed her
for her summoning.

Part II - Dreams & Realizations

Albatross

The world is burning
I soar
Above the molten landscape below
Above the evermore faint
Cries of the dying

I drift
Charting the divide
Between heaven and earth
Wondering
How long I must stay aloft
The world is burning

What Lies Beneath

What a delicate
sweet
pursuit.
Searching tangled wired connections.
Snipping the wires
MACHINE NO!
Dismantled?
Yes.
Playful yank on reluctant bolt.
Removing plates
put there by a bastard God of society
for its protection
not mine.
Mine
this organic rot that dies with me
this humanity
this love
is worth all of the skyscrapers in Hell.
No matter how long they stand.

Between Sunset and Dawn

I like sunsets and dawn
when light is softened
after having to travel further than planned
through the atmosphere
picking up indiscretions from dust-motes
and butterflies
illuminating the world from an angle
revealing so much that would be washed out
by the full glare of day
I prefer to live a life
that is equal parts light
and
darkness

Bottoming Out

Looking into a mine shaft
How deep?
A rock is tossed in.
I am that rock
falling through utter night
suspended
waiting for an impact
that never seems to come.
I have been falling so long
there is no up or down
I am
still.
It is the world that whistles past
faster
ever faster.
I am still.
Everything is falling past me.
If I try to grasp at anything
the force
would tear my arms off.
So
let go.
Letgoletgoletgoletgo.
And
be still.

Small Craft

I am a small craft
fashioned of muted light
fading in
and out
of visibility
in the mist of a dream
I skim the surface
of a collective subconscious
too deep
to measure.

Dreams

I love my dreams
all of them
even ones where I fight nightmares
I run
I fight
I fuck

Every day for the last month
I have gone to bed
early
so impatient to dream
that it keeps me awake.

Wake child

Wake child
and look around you.
You dreamed a dream that many call a nightmare
but
let it be.
Dreams and reality are so confusing.
Don't you agree?
But then again
it is all so simple
you just open your eyes
and see.
Let us say you choose your place to be.
Wake child
and look around you
at your new reality.

A Moment Only

My dreams are lost
within my dreams
that I desperately try to grasp
And so I try
to live my dreams
that last a moment only.
Moments
in each a life
that passes
never slowly
but often
so very often
lonely.

Heaven

I am on a roadway
carved into a cliff-side
and engulfed in thunder

across the chasm
I see
the wind
chasing rainbows
up a waterfall that fills
my entire field of vision
from horizon to horizon
with falling water

a titanic sight

an oceans' worth of water
tumbling over the edge
every
minute

islands of rock
extend out from its face
entire forests appearing diminutive
on their peaks

as I lean across the stonework
at the edge of the cliff
I realize
I'm in some version of Heaven

in this incredible thunder
the sight
the vibration
of these falls
I lose my identity

my sense
of myself

suddenly
I'm a spectator
in wooden bleachers
watching small racecars
tear around a short-track
their engines screaming
their drivers ecstatic

they can race
as fast as they want
and never die

someone turns to me
knowingly
and yells
over the thunder of the race

there are as many Heavens
as there are people to imagine them
all right here for us to explore

as long as your sense
of identity & need
is too small
to contain the real you
the you
that exists
beyond this reality
you'll never find the real Heaven

until
you quit wanting any Heaven
until
you can realize
that you
are just
a small
part
of God's mind
separated from God
for God's own entertainment

Heaven is
re-merging
with your own greater self

you can enter the real Heaven
when you lose this
your sense of identity
and need

In Heaven
you lose yourself
and
you're not there to know it.

Santa Dream

I'm lost in a whiteout,
where fog and snow steal the horizon,
and all things change,
distance,
perspective,
size,
all become abstractions.

I walk on.
It's hard to tell time.
Eyes down, watching my feet shuffle
on the flat ice

I feel compelled to look up, and see them
massive beasts
heavy muzzles
shaggy, with a forest of up-curved antlers
on their collective heads.

I slowly walk the line of them.
Steam from their breath
steam rising from their backs
the smell of grass and manure
in this, until now, almost sterile
environment.

I warm my numbing hands on their flanks,
they follow me with their eyes until I pass,
then merely stand drowsily
in place.

The sled, also,
is large and clumsy-looking.
A flat oaken platform,

each plank quietly displaying the pattern
hewn by the hand-axe
that formed them.

I think
perhaps the reindeer know the way out.
I stand on the sled since it has no seat.
I wonder where the owner is.
I shout "Hey!"
and the animals lunge forward, quickly breaking
into a leaping gallop.
I get up from the tarp-covered load.
The ice hisses by for hours.
There is no horizon.
No sun.

Then
the sound of the ice is gone
nothing else is changed.
It would be silent but for the sound of reindeer,
huffing,
surging,
and farting
when they nip at each other.

There are no reins.
What use are they,
when you don't know where you're going?
Unless you want to stop.
I can't stop.

The ice suddenly becomes black and reflective.
The mist scatters into clouds at the edge of my vision.
And the stars hang over my head
in a frozen
crystal rain.

Oh it's cold
and oh it's sweet
and I yell again and race over a frozen sea.
It must be, for there is light below me.
Vast carpets of twinkling color
that call to me from the depths.
I know it must be plankton
but I allow myself to think,
in this vast, empty place
that I am really flying,
and that the lights are cities
far, far below.

Looking under the tarp, I see tools
and the sled's load.
It looks like sand.
I don't want to tire the animals
so I grab a small, flat shovel, and start flinging
sand over the side.

And as it scatters it catches the starlight
and then seems to drop
straight through the ice.
As if it weren't there
spiraling slowly down to kiss the city lights below.
And the sled grows lighter and faster,
and I roar and laugh
with hope that I will see the grass where the
reindeer eat.
Hope that I will live and find warmth and food,
that instead of dying cold and alone I will have a
chance to grow old,
surrounded by people I love as I fling more sand
each individual grain symbolizes hope

each a falling star
one to match
every light below and more.

If you were real, city,
I think to myself,
I would wish the same for you.

In the Mist

Last night I dreamed
I had returned to Humboldt County.
Years pass, and I find myself rowing
through coastal fog
threading my way through titanic snags,
twenty feet through the center.

A dense crown of branches
three times as thick as my body,
bleached white, reaches up to claw holes in the
mist.

My oars quietly splash,
I hear the cries of flocks of floating puffins,
and the occasional loon.

I ready a drop-line.
It is easy to catch very large rock cod here
because commercial boats would lose their gear
in tangled branches
that still exist going hundreds of feet down.

Redwoods still grow and tower over me
in the thinning coastal fog.
I see them on shore, poking up from the mist,
just as these do from the water.

I tie my double-ended skiff to one of the nearby
branches
spreading into a dead, 30-foot crown.
I nestle down into the depression in its center,
hold still, and listen
to the birds and the waves massaging the shore.

Prelude to Laughing Buddha

We have a lot of dreams that are transient
eyelid-theater
our sub-conscious entertaining itself

Other dreams
I feel
come from outside of me
I call them God-dreams
I can tell the difference easily because
I remember God-dreams

They have some kind of message for me

This is one of those dreams

Laughing Buddha

One night
I dreamed I lived in old India
I was a middle-class merchant
living well
indulging myself

I had nice rooms on an upper story

I'd look out through the carved screens on my
windows
and watch the business of the city go by in the
street below me

and every once in a while I'd see a man standing
on a corner

He was a Laughing Buddha
a religious figure:
shaved head
and his robes
and his great smile

they always called these kind of men the Laughing
Buddhas.
They always had a crowd around them
and they were always laughing
and enjoying each other's company.

And I was rather lonely
I'd look down at all this activity
and think my wealth wasn't really that great...
I'd like to be like him
and one day
I decided I would

So I bought the clothes
and shaved my head
looked in the mirror
and there
was a Laughing Buddha

I went out on the street
it was like I was a different person

I could tell stories
and meet people.
We laughed
and enjoyed each other
and I was having a great time.

As I walked along
I came to where a prince and his family were eating
in their little alcove next to the street
it was just a little carved wooden barrier
between them and the people passing by.
The prince looked at me walking by and said
come eat with us

so I joined them

and one of his favorite wives
was passing me little bits of food
and we're laughing and talking

and all of a sudden
I felt overcome with guilt.
I was being treated
with a respect I hadn't earned
and so I told the prince

I—I—
I have to tell you:

I'm not really a Laughing Buddha
I'm just...
pretending to be one

And as his wife
continues to feed me little delicacies
the prince laughs
and says

well you're dressed like one
so you're halfway there.

...the scene of the dream changes...

it's late at night

it's cold
and I'm discovering
that my Laughing Buddha robe
isn't as warm as it could be

I'm wandering up a very
narrow
canyon
and there's only a little strip of stars overhead
as the walls
grow closer and closer together
and it's getting very dark
and very cold
and I'm carrying a little lantern
and all of a sudden I come to a rockslide blocking
my progress through this little canyon
and I don't know what to do

I can't go forward

I'm cold
and tired

and far from any kind of shelter
so I put my lantern on a rock
and I start crying.

Then a woman's voice
as clear as small bells ringing
so beautiful that I dare not turn around
to look
to see who it comes from
because I know that kind of beauty would destroy
me.
The voice says
well
you've been praying to me
so you're halfway there

Part III - Frustrations, Desires & Intimacies

Bus Stop

Twelve-thirty A.M.
The small shelter provides
little of that,
its windows broken by vandals.
We sit
bundled in coats and sweaters
insulated against the cold
and each other,
sitting apart on the damp bench
looking for images in our clouded breath
and finding none.
The bus is always late
the street is unrecognizable
in its emptiness
populated only
by the reflected echoes of street lights
and us.
Your face is the only spot of warmth
a banked fire
trying to burn until morning.
The bus is twenty minutes late
It roars up in the night's shattered silence
you scramble inside
the brilliant island of glaring light
sound
movement.
Our obligatory hug
forgotten in the frantic search for change
then
the street is empty
but for me.

Moon Walk

The vacuum between us
would suck my lungs out
if I were not protected

Touching you
feels
as if I wear an EVA suit
so many layers between us

Kissing you
is like trying to penetrate
bulletproof glass
with my lips

Cupid

Cupid isn't a fat little boy
With a toy bow
I've seen him
I search for him
At least
Now I do
He looks Roman
More than Greek
Barrel chest
Powerful shoulders
He carries a short
Curved bow
That looks difficult to draw
In a small
Plain quiver
He carries obsidian-tipped arrows.

The first time I saw him
Was out of the corner of my eye
Just before I lost all sense
Of reality
I woke to the world
With a blank spot
In my memory
In my heart
And I was alone
And it hurt real bad
And it happened again
And again
Until I grew weary
And learned to avoid
Hard-driven arrows

And merely suffer
Minor blood loss
Instead.

I've had an idea
The painful thing
About being shot by Cupid
Is being alone
When I wake up
I stalk Cupid
I watch
Quietly
As Cupid enters the forest
The sun
Briefly dappling
His back
His golden hair
I stalk him
The ruler of this domain
Of love
As he stalks others
As they are transformed
And lost
I will cheat Cupid
And someone
For once
Won't go through the pain
Of falling in love
And waking up alone.

Second Coming

Let me see you
as the Anti-Life Cathedrals burst into flame.
Let me see you.
You,
with a naked life-lust.
Dancing your love
as you greedily copulate in the grass
as you transform passion
into the gentle religion of life.

Kali

I kiss her fiercely
She will accept it no other way
coming away in a state of arousal
with blood in my mouth from mashing my teeth,
passion I had forgotten
consuming love
that leaves nothing behind
but a pile of smoking bones
and memories.
True love.
Devastating love.
Liberating me from the limitations
of my mind
that I may experience in the infinite
which has lain
just out of my reach.
Beauty and decay
growth and decadence
two sides of the same golden coin.
Value beyond measure.

Too Young

She was so waif-like
innocent and vulnerable
with her dark eyes
and the glint of crystals and Ju-Ju charms
hanging from her
ever so delicate
neck.
Multi-jeweled fingers
danced on the counter
as she displayed treasures
fetched from secret places.
She felt to me like
a small animal
that would eat from my hand
if only
I could hold still enough.

Lady Aurora

I think of you
in the night
your dress
smoke
revealing
veiling
your sweet
strong
body
as you dance
light and shadow
eyes lifted
your dark hair
a leaf-strewn cloud
all striving
towards hidden stars
dancing
the language of Gods.

Sea King

If I were a Sea King
I'd sit on a throne of inlaid stone
and whale bone
I'd raid the city you live in
and sail you here
a thousand leagues from your home.
I'd dress you in silks, gold and amber
I'd dress you like a bride.
And every month I'd raise your ransom
so more time could be stolen
to keep you
by my side.
We would never be apart
I'm sure
before long you'd realize
though I'd stolen you
you had stolen
my heart.

I'd go with you
to your father's land
and willingly
risk his wrath.
And risk the greater danger
of you lying
that after you were safe
you would look at me
and laugh.
I'd hold your hand for safety
walking down the crowded court
going to see your father
a real king

to find out if my life would be long
or short.
To be a Sea King
it's only a dream.
I'm really only an ordinary man
exactly what I seem.
But my love for you
is as real as day.
I couldn't really think
how to tell you
so I chose this
roundabout way.

Sunshine

The morning light is kind to your face
glowing with warmth
like curtains of lace.
And I wish that my mornings would always be so
your soft gentle features
and the sunshine's soft glow.
Even when the sky is covered
and we see the sun no more
I will look in your eyes
and glimpse the sky
and know what a woman is for.

Pan

It was twilight
when I woke on the beach
with sand in my mouth
and started to shiver
while I groped
for the half-empty wine jug

Feeling the new sunburn
pull tight on my shoulders
I saw glimmers of light
dancing under the trees
rising naked
hooves clattering on slippery river stone
I fall and hear laughter
get up
and fall again
tripping over my erection
stumbling
into the forest.

I laugh too drunk now on wine and dreams
chasing moonlit shadows
just out of reach
but
dancing with them still
until
exhausted
my face whipped by branches and brush
I break into the open
and lay down by the river
panting
as the full moon
crawls to bed in the treetops.

Kindled

Let me inhale this light you breathe
let it wend its way
into my heart
and kindle so much wood
into flame.
Let me be consumed
from my bones to my skin
so that I glow
like a paper lantern.
I would be
quietly carried away by the wind
to become
a distant point of light
one of many
in a starry sky.

Wet Dream

When I was a fisherman,
we would shut the boat down
and drift at night while we slept,
waking periodically to look at the radar
to make sure we didn't run into anyone.

Like a 15-foot-tall roller coaster
in slow motion,
we would climb to the top of the rolling swells
And then sliiiiiiiide slowly down the other side to
the trough.

I frequently wished I had a woman with me,
so I could use the iron-hard erection
the sensual ocean's movement had induced in me.
I just wanted to be holding on to her,
joined together,
and let Mother Ocean move us in our embrace.

Touch

I touch
without touching you
I kiss
without kissing you
I love
without possessing you

I step into the space
you have just left
and merge
with the still beating
after image
of your heart

I Want to Be

I want to be your pit bull
your tarnished knight.
I write poems about you
and read them
only to strangers.
No one
should know they are loved
that much.

I See You Clearly

You stand
Shining
From internal combustion
I circle you
A planetary body
Succumbing to your gravitational pull
I hold you
Unable to bear
The sight of your tears
I close my eyes
But see you clearly
Still

Love

Love
I have found that
my pain
is permeable only to love.
Love
as I grow older
mellower
there is more love in me.
It lives in my belly.
As my capacity for love grows
so does my belly!
I am SO FULL OF IT!!!

Part IV - Dance of Life

Last Dance

Dance
and learn your limitations
dance
even if no one else
would call that
dance
dance
as if
this were your last
dance

dance

Thank You

Thank you
for touching me gently
sometimes
my cracks
are full thickness
and all that holds me together
is a thin
porcelain
glaze.
Though cast
in the shape of a dragon
you are kind enough
to handle me
as if I were
an ancient artifact.

Your Dance

Your dance
creates a power
as inexorable as a glacier
nothing
can stand up to your beauty
you move mountains
as easily as breathing
I want to fall into you
and preserve this moment for centuries.

Piece of Glass

I am just a piece of glass
I spent my early life
lying at the side of the road
puncturing bicycle tires
later
I fell into the ocean
then
was thrown back on the shore
sharp edges softened
my surfaces
frosted.
We are all old enough
to have been broken many times
together
in this dance
we merge
and scatter
and combine into random patterns
that are never repeated.
We are God's kaleidoscope
we amuse him
when he is not busy
doing other
esoteric things.

If God Were Deaf

I think of God
as a man
sitting on an endless beach
the sound of prayers
rising from the Earth
like a flock of seabirds.
When you dance
your spirit shines
with the pulse
and intensity
of a lighthouse.
Even if God were deaf
your prayer
would get through to him.

Waves

Today I was a rock
The people I danced with
Waves

To a rock
Days and seasons
Are a heartbeat

Waves
Sometimes
Cover me
Engulf me
As if to consume me

Eventually
I will be reduced to sand
Running through your fingers
Like water

Light and Dark Dance Under the Mountain

How did I come to be here
at this dance under the mountain?
Strange creatures here
fragile or strong
figures of light meet those of darkness.
Veiled or naked
all have one thing in common—
they are not afraid.

I am.
What should they fear
if not me?
Why are they unafraid?

I can bear no iron here.
Armor and sword left at the door
leave me naked.
Who would fear a man
bereft of his
hard
sharp
edges?

I watch the transformation.
They descend underground
finding light where others see darkness.
Shoulders straighten
steps quicken
they dance.

Light and darkness
naked or veiled
there is no shame.
This is that place

where
words unspoken
can still be heard
emotions unshared
are still felt.

Warmth becomes heat
motion blurs
touch becomes connection
like the light of an expanding universe
love becomes blinding
till there can be no more dances.

A bottle or a wooden cup
each is just a container that can hold so much
and no more.
I am full.
I too can hold no more.

This is what lies underneath.
The magic most men never see.
Not because it is invisible
but because it is denied by them.

All dances come to an end.
I watch the transformation in reverse
the figures of light
resume their worldly identities
and
climb the stairs to the street above them.

And I
am left alone in the dark.

A darkness punctuated by memories
intimacies

like flashbulbs in an unlit room.
like lightning
charging the air with ozone.

And I
am left alone in the dark.

Author's Acknowledgements

So many people have encouraged me, for which I am deeply grateful. Special thanks go to Briana Barrett-Squirrel, Phil Bevis, and Annie Brulé, who have sometimes guided and sometimes herded me to complete this book.

To my friends at dance, thank you for giving me life.

Ron Ellison, February 2015

About the Author

Ron Ellison's journey began in harsh poverty. He has been a lumberjack, draft resister, art student, bum, soldier, fisherman, nurse specializing in acute psychiatric and drug cases, artist, and writer. He lives in Seattle.

CPSIA information can be obtained
at www.ICGtesting.com
Printed in the USA
FSOW01n1423010515
6861FS